Police Horse

by Susan McCloskey
photographed by Kevin Brusie

MODERN CURRICULUM PRESS
Pearson Learning Group

Meet Spree. Spree works for the police department in Portland, Maine. Officer Lisa Sweat works with him. They're partners.

It takes about two hours for Spree and Officer Lisa to get ready for work.

First Officer Lisa washes Spree. Next she feeds him and cleans his stall. Then she saddles him. Finally, she puts on her uniform.

Then they're ready to ride the streets of Portland. They have serious work to do.

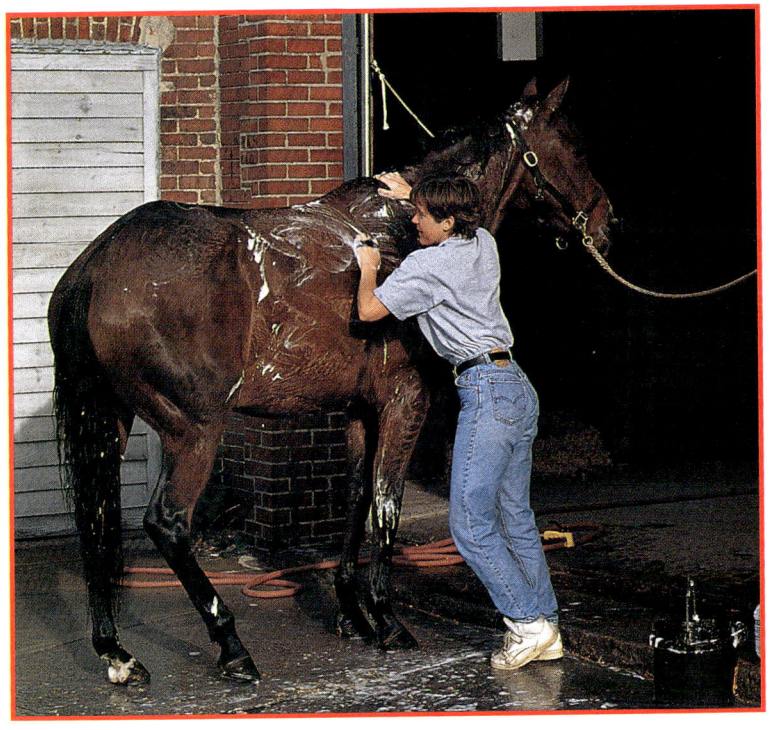

Spree and Officer Lisa stand out in a crowd. That's good. There is less likely to be a problem when people know a police officer is near.

But Spree and Officer Lisa always have to be ready, just in case. Once they saw a shoplifter run out of a store. They chased him down a street that was being fixed.

Workers and trucks were everywhere. A police car couldn't have gone there. But Spree could. And guess what? They got the shoplifter.

Their work can be dangerous. Once Officer Lisa and another horse were hit by a car. (Luckily, they were okay.) Another officer on horseback chased the car through the neighborhood. The driver did not get away.

Speeding cars! Noisy people! Horns! They can be frightening. And they're all part of life in the city.

How did Spree learn not to be frightened? By going to school! Spree spent two months learning about city life. He had to prove he could stay calm. He had to get used to noise and other city things like balloons and flags!

On the job, Spree had to learn something else—trust.

Spree doesn't like walking through puddles. He can't tell how deep they are. But he will walk through them for Officer Lisa. He trusts her. He knows she wouldn't ask him to do anything that would hurt him.

Officer Lisa has learned about Spree too. She can tell how he feels by his "body language."

Spree's work is not all serious. Part of his job is to make friends for the police. That's easy! Just seeing him makes people smile.

Sometimes a friend gives Spree his favorite snack—carrots!

Sometimes Spree and Officer Lisa work with Kookie and another officer. Officer Lisa says that Spree and Kookie act "like kids in the back seat of a car." (What do you think she means by that?)

Sometimes Spree works at night. He and Officer Lisa keep an eye on crowds of summer visitors to Portland. The crowds can be noisy. Spree has to have steady nerves.

Spree does a lot of walking on stony streets, so he needs strong, healthy feet. Every six weeks Spree gets new shoes.

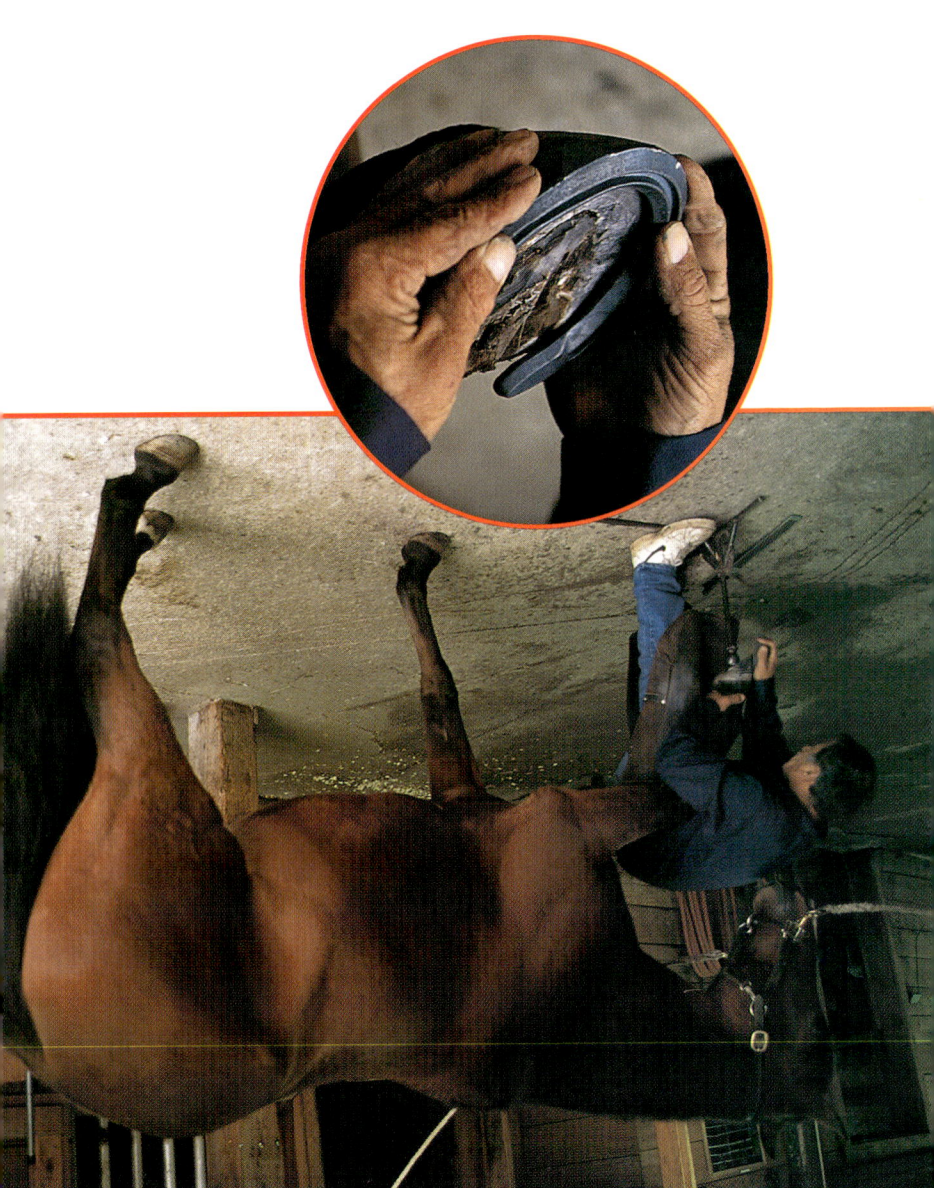

Winters in Portland are cold. The streets are covered with snow and ice. Slippery streets are a problem for Spree. So when winter comes, Spree and Officer Lisa say good-by. Then Officer Lisa rides in a police car for a few months. Spree takes a vacation at a nearby farm.

But it's too soon to think about winter. Now, during the golden days of autumn, Spree and Officer Lisa are happy. They both love working together to keep the streets safe.